FRIEDA MAKES A DIFFERENCE

FRIEDA MAKES A DIFFERENCE

The Sustainable Development Goals and How You Too Can Change the World

UNITED NATIONS

ACKNOWLEDGEMENTS

This book was originally conceived and published by the United Nations Information Centre (UNIC) in Windhoek, Namibia—one of the branch offices of the United Nations Department of Global Communications. The idea behind this book was to help young readers relate to and better understand the Sustainable Development Goals.

UN Publications would like to acknowledge and thank the following people for bringing this story to life and into children's hands around the world: Anthea Basson, the National Information Officer and Head of UNIC Windhoek, and Welda Mouton, the Public Information Assistant.

The story was written by Nicola Gallagher, a communications professional. Illustrations were created by Nelett Loubser, the owner of KunsHuis Graphic Design.

For more information about the UNIC Windhoek, visit http://windhoek.sites.unicnetwork.org.

For more information about the Sustainable Development Goals, visit www.un.org/sustainabledevelopment.

United Nations Publications
405 East 42nd Street, S-09FW001
New York, NY 10017
USA

Email: publications@un.org
Website: shop.un.org

ISBN (paperback): 9789211014068
ISBN (hardback): 9789211014099
eISBN: 9789210040495
ePub ISBN: 9789213582763

A NOTE TO OUR READERS

On 1 January 2016, 17 Sustainable Development Goals, also known as the SDGs, officially came into force. These goals are part of a plan of action that world leaders agreed will help make the world a better place by 2030.

The year 2030 may seem far away, but it takes a lot of work and commitment to solve these problems – such as ending poverty, fighting inequality, tackling climate change, protecting our oceans and animals, and ensuring that no one is left behind.

The Goals call for all countries to help protect our planet. This includes governments, businesses, civil society and young people like you! In this book you will learn more about what the Goals are and also find some tips on what you can do to make a difference in your life and in the lives of those around you! Making a difference starts with you!

In the land of the free is where Frieda plays.
Her country is so beautiful, in many different ways.

Breathtaking landscapes, and animals galore;

Plus kind people, tasty food, fun music, and more.

In school Frieda learns about the countries of the world. She learns about the United Nations, and how countries work together to create peace. The UN works with governments to make the world an even better place, for all people, no matter their gender, religion or race.

One day, a woman named Ana from the United Nations visits Frieda's school. The smart children answer Ana's tough questions about what the United Nations does.

Hearing more about the United Nations motivates Frieda to grow up and change the world. However, she thinks that right now she can't because she is only a little girl.

Ana tells her,
"You can bring about change! There's a lot of
things you can do, a very wide range!"

"The United Nations is working to achieve the Sustainable Development Goals. Everyone can help to achieve them; young or old; no matter their roles."

"Starting off with achieving no poverty,
we must work to meet our basic need.

Everyone deserves a safe home;
this is something we need, indeed!"

"Next, we want zero hunger and for all people to have access to food.

Nutritious meals help you to perform well and put you in a good mood."

"Everyone has the right to medicine,
being able to exercise and good health;

Regardless of where you live,
your age or your wealth."

"It is important to learn how to read and write and how to do math.

All people deserve quality education so that they can succeed on their life path."

"All boys and girls should be treated equally and given the same opportunities.

We must promote equality in all of
our communities."

"Everyone has the right to clean
water and sanitation;

In the North, South, East and West,
all people of every nation."

"Instead of using petrol and other resources that can be depleted,

Sunlight can power things, and its use can be repeated and repeated."

"Work should be safe, secure, and fair.

Good jobs and good pay for everyone, everywhere."

"Our roads and bridges should be built to last and be strong.

So that when traveling, all people can be safe and nothing will go wrong."

"Everyone should
be treated right
and with equality,

All people deserve
a life of the highest
quality."

"As the population grows, cities also need to grow in the right way.

They need safe buildings and places for everyone to stay."

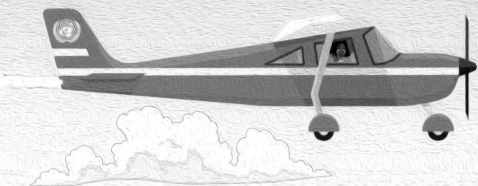

11 SUSTAINABLE CITIES
AND COMMUNITIES

"We must be responsible when we use things, to this we must commit! You can recycle, reuse and reduce to achieve it!"

"The world is warmer. The climate is changing. This we know is true.

So reduce pollution. Take action now.
There's so much we can do!"

13 CLIMATE ACTION

"The fish in the ocean need to be protected, too.

Preventing overfishing is
what we can do."

"Lions, rhinos, and elephants are some animals that live on land.

We must help to protect them.
We must take a stand."

"We must strive for peace, justice and strong institutions.

COURT OF JUSTICE

To ensure that all people are protected and treated fairly, we must find solutions!"

"Finally, everyone must work together to make the world much better for all."

Frieda was so happy to learn that the
Sustainable Development Goals are
something she can take part in.

That night, Frieda hurries home to spend time with her family.

She tells them how the United Nations is changing the world and how she wants to change it, too.

Frieda says, "Let's put our heads together! Everyone! You and me!"

"BECAUSE TOGETHER WE CAN MAKE A DIFFERENCE!"

WHAT YOU CAN DO

✓ Turn off the lights when you're not in the room. Unplug appliances when you're not using them.

✓ Bring your own bag when you shop. You won't need a plastic bag from a store if you carry your own reusable bag.

✓ Recycle paper, plastic, glass and aluminum to help stop landfills from growing.

✓ Bike, walk or take public transport. Save the car trips for when you've got a big group.

✓ Adjust your thermostat: lower in the winter, higher in the summer.

✓ Donate what you don't use. Local charities will give your gently used clothes, books and furniture a new life.

✓ Go to a local polling station when there are elections. Find out who is trying to make a difference.

✓ Invite people to speak to your class about how they are helping your community become a better place (then thank them!).

✓ Volunteer in your neighborhood. You don't have to go far to find ways to help others.

✓ Talk to your family about what you can all do to make a difference where you live.

RESOURCES

Visit these websites to learn about simple actions you can take in your daily life to make a difference. If you care about the future, be the change!

The Lazy Person's Guide to Saving the World by the United Nations tells us global citizens what we can do to affect change. Some tips are simple and you may already be doing them. Others will require you to change or adopt new habits.

www.un.org/sustainabledevelopment/takeaction

Everyone can drive the change. With #YouNeedtoKnow, pick one of the 170 simple actions and contribute to making the world a better place – one step at a time! Resources are available in eight languages.

www.youneedtoknow.ch

This book was printed on FSC Mixed paper using soy based ink.